FIRST CONTACT

a brief treatment for young substance users

The *First Contact* program was developed and written by:
Curtis Breslin
Kathy Sdao-Jarvie
Elsbeth Tupker
Shelly Pearlman

Centre
for Addiction and
Mental Health
Centre de
toxicomanie et
de santé mentale

A Pan American Health Organization /
World Health Organization Collaborating Centre

First Contact
A Brief Treatment for Young Substance Users

For information on other Centre for Addiction and Mental Health resource materials or to place an order, please contact:

Marketing and Sales Services
Centre for Addiction and Mental Health
33 Russell Street
Toronto, Ontario
Canada M5S 2S1
Tel.: 1-800-661-1111 or 416-595-6059 in Toronto
E-mail: marketing@camh.net

Web site: www.camh.net

2268 REV / 07-03   PG098

Disponible en français sous le titre
Premier contact : Traitement de courte durée
pour les jeunes usagers d'alcool et de drogues

Acknowledgments

The project team would like to thank the following people for their valuable advice and assistance in the development of this treatment manual and the clinical materials:

The *First Contact* program was developed and written by:
Curtis Breslin
Kathy Sdao-Jarvie
Elsbeth Tupker
Shelly Pearlman

With help from:
Joanne Shenfeld
Colleen Kelly
Farzana Doctor
Gloria Chaim
Kathryn Baverstock
Selina Li
Virginia Ittig-Deland
Bruce Ballon

Youth Advisory Team:
Carina Cucci
Gitan Ramjee
Stephanie Randall
Christie Thickett
Holly Trimnell
Paul Bruno

Copy editing:
Sue McCluskey

Manual development, design and production:
Julia Greenbaum
Nancy Leung
Eva Katz
Mary Quartarone

Evaluation Team:
Selina Li
Virginia Ittig-Deland

Ontario Youth Managers Co-ordinating Group, Advisory Committee:
Jean Gagné, *Maison Fraternité, Vanier*
Ellie Jenks, *CHOICES: Drug and Alcohol Counselling for Youth, Owen Sound*
Dave Roy, *CHOICES: Drug and Alcohol Counselling for Youth, Owen Sound*
Mary Nemeth, *Haldimand-Norfolk Addiction Services, Simcoe*
Bob Pollack, *Addiction Assessment Service of Ottawa-Carleton, Ottawa*
Peter McKenna, *Addiction Assessment Service of Ottawa-Carleton, Ottawa*
Paul Welsh, *Rideauwood Addiction and Family Services, Ottawa*
Joan Leadbeater-Graham, *Rideauwood Addiction and Family Services, Ottawa*
Diane Walker, *Smith Alcohol and Drug Dependency Clinic, Thunder Bay*

Field Test Sites:
Addiction Research Foundation Youth Program, now a division of the Centre for Addiction and Mental Health
Addiction Assessment Service of Ottawa-Carleton
Maison Fraternité

Comments on drafts were received from:
Jean Gagné
Clara Panarella
Bob Pollack
Marilyn Herie
Lynn Watkin-Merek
Marla Banning
Andrew Drake
Kathy Kilburn
Darryl Upfold
Jane Fjeld

Core Project Team:
Curtis Breslin
Elsbeth Tupker
Kathy Sdao-Jarvie
Shelly Pearlman
Julia Greenbaum

Contents

Acknowledgments

About the program 1

  Introduction 1

    What is *First Contact?* 1

    Why is there a need for a brief treatment for youth? 1

    Who will use this manual? 2

    Who is the *First Contact* program appropriate for? 3

  Elements of *First Contact* 3

    Conceptual basis 3

    Therapeutic style 4

Treatment sessions 7

  About the clinical materials 7

  Giving personalized feedback at assessment 9

    Personalized feedback on substance use and consequences 11

  Session 1: Decision to change 23

    The role of the counsellor. 25

    Breaking the ice, establishing group cohesion and group rules 25

    Decision to change. 26

    Goal setting 26

  Session 2: Triggers, consequences and alternatives 37

    Check-in 39

    Exploring patterns of use 39

    Strategies for change 40

  Session 3: Things that are important to me 47

    Check-in 49

    Life goals and values 49

  Session 4: Stages of change 59

    Review of change process 61

    Treatment needs and options for the future. 61

References 67

About the program

Introduction

WHAT IS *FIRST CONTACT*?

First Contact is a brief treatment program designed for adolescent and young adult substance users. It is an outpatient program that combines elements of cognitive-behavioural and Motivational Interviewing approaches. The program can be a "first step" for youth with substance use problems, fostering motivation for change before addressing more specialized or long-term needs.

The program can also serve as a "stand-alone" intervention for those youth who need short-term assistance to change or for youth who may only attend a few sessions because they terminate treatment early. As in motivational interventions for adults with drinking problems (e.g., Motivational Enhancement Therapy; Miller et al., 1995), the goals in *First Contact* are to evoke statements of problem perception from the clients, help clients resolve ambivalence towards change, and help clients mobilize their own skills and resources for change.

The program includes normative feedback, given at assessment, regarding the extent and consequences of clients' substance use as compared to other young people in Canada, four outpatient sessions, delivered in either an individual or a group format, and in-session exercises that cover topics such as:

- discussing costs and benefits of changing
- setting substance use goals and monitoring results

- discussing what went well or not-so-well in the past week
- discussing life goals and how substance use affects achieving these goals
- identifying high-risk situations for alcohol or drug use
- developing strategies and problem-solving skills to find alternatives to substance use
- learning about the change process and how to sustain change over time, as well as coping with relapse
- "next step" planning for the client.

WHY IS THERE A NEED FOR A BRIEF TREATMENT FOR YOUTH?

Most young people tend to drop out early from extended outpatient treatment for substance use. For example, at an adolescent outpatient program in the U.S., 70 per cent of the clients left before the end of the program (Lawendowski, 1998). These numbers are similar in Canada, where Ontario youth treatment agencies report that clients attended an average of four outpatient sessions before leaving the program. This means that many youth receive brief treatment regardless of the intentions of the counsellor or program.

Willingness to change, and ambivalence about their drug use, clearly contributes to the rate of treatment dropout of young substance users. An initial intervention that engages youth in treatment and addresses ambivalence about change would be a useful component within the continuum of care for this population.

Currently, 18 of 20 controlled trials show that many adult problem drinkers respond well to brief treatment interventions (Miller, 1999). It is reasonable to expect that adapting these brief interventions to the youth population will also provide a useful treatment option.

Young substance abusers differ from adults in several ways. Youth clients use multiple substances and present with multiple life problems more often than adult clients. Many are pressured by parents and the law to attend treatment, creating a situation where they are resistant and unmotivated. However, because brief interventions emphasize non-confrontation, self-reliance and personal choice, this approach may be well suited to helping clients express and resolve their ambivalence about change.

Early results have been promising. (Lawendowski, 1998; Wilkinson & Martin, 1983). For example, Lawendowski (1998) conducted a single assessment and feedback session, based on the Motivational Interviewing (MI) approach, with adolescents about to start outpatient substance abuse treatment. (MI is a key element of the *First Contact* program that is described later in the manual.) Six months after that session, data showed that adolescents who received this motivational session attended more outpatient sessions and reported less heavy substance use than adolescents not receiving the MI session.

At the field test of *First Contact* at two test sites in Ottawa, the program was well received by the counsellors and over 30 clients who participated. Further, a six-month evaluation follow-up conducted at the Centre for Addiction and Mental Health shows that, of the 45 clients followed to date, two-thirds reported significant reductions in number of days of use. These clients also reported a 50 per cent decrease in number of substance-related consequences six months after treatment. Taken together, this evidence provides preliminary support for motivational interventions to assist young substance users in the change process.

WHO WILL USE THIS MANUAL?

The manual is for counsellors who specialize in treating young substance users. Although counsellors in other settings, such as mental health and social services, may have the generic counselling skills and knowledge that are essential for a program such as *First Contact*, additional knowledge and skills specific to treating substance use are also needed to implement this program. The counsellor intending to use this program should be familiar with the theory and practice of Motivational Interviewing (Miller & Rollnick, 1991) and the cognitive-behavioural strategies associated with relapse prevention (Marlatt & Gordon, 1985).

In addition to these more general approaches to substance use treatment, counsellors must also be familiar with assessment and treatment issues concerning adolescent substance use, which are discussed in *Youth And Drugs: An Education Package for Professionals* (Addiction Research Foundation, 1991). If the program is used in a group format, the counsellor needs to be familiar with group skills, such as building cohesion.

First Contact does not include a formal drug education session because the program's focus is primarily therapeutic, not educational. Instead, *First Contact* provides information and a context for youth to examine the impact that drug use is having on their lives. However, counsellors will need to know about the short- and long-term effects of commonly used drugs. At times, clients may have misconceptions about drug effects, and will need accurate information. Opportunities to discuss misconceptions can occur during the feedback at assessment, and also during the in-session exercises (e.g., **Decision to Change**). In addition, drug information pamphlets can be made available to youth both at assessment and throughout the sessions.

If, as part of a continuum of services for substance use treatment, a drug education program is also available, this could be provided as a separate component. Further care or treatment after completion of *First Contact* could also include:

- outpatient, day or residential substance abuse treatment
- family therapy
- continuing care
- therapies for concurrent mental health problems
- anger management
- stress management
- leisure counselling
- social skills training
- vocational counselling.

WHO IS THE *FIRST CONTACT* PROGRAM APPROPRIATE FOR?

First Contact has been developed for youth between the ages of 14 and 20 years with substance abuse problems, for whom outpatient treatment is thought to be appropriate. This program is not intended for youth who are in crisis or in need of hospitalization for medical conditions (e.g., serious withdrawal symptoms) or who have serious psychiatric concurrent disorders. Results of the ongoing evaluation of *First Contact* will provide more information on its utility with certain types of clients, such as those who are legally mandated.

Through field testing and focus groups with counsellors working with youth, clinical materials have been developed or adapted for this age group. An advisory committee of young people also played an active role in developing the *First Contact* program. Involvement of youth in the early phase of development helped ensure that the ideas and words used in the materials are relevant and age-appropriate.

Although *First Contact* is designed to be helpful to a broad range of young substance users, most clients will also have other treatment needs, such as anger management skills or family counselling. If these needs are not of an urgent nature, our suggestion is to complete the program materials before focusing on clients' more specialized needs. The reasoning behind this recommendation is that, as stated earlier, youth clients tend to drop out of treatment programs, so the *First Contact* program's topics are designed to strengthen clients' motivation and commitment to change. This, in turn, may have an impact on clients' interest in additional interventions following *First Contact*. Also, retaining the overall structure of *First Contact* provides a clear agreement with the client on the number of sessions. A program that is both well defined and limited in duration may help enhance the clients' commitment to the entire treatment process.

Elements of First Contact

CONCEPTUAL BASIS

Guided Self-Change program

Many of the exercises in *First Contact* are influenced by the Guided Self-Change (GSC) program (Sobell & Sobell, 1993). GSC is a brief outpatient treatment designed for adults who have mild to moderate alcohol and drug problems. A key characteristic of GSC is that people take major responsibility for their own treatment, including setting substance use goals and taking action towards achieving those goals. Personalized feedback, readings and homework help clients to:

- examine the pros and cons of changing and strengthen their commitment to change
- identify situations that put them at high risk for use
- develop strategies to deal with these situations and plan specific steps to change their use.

Consistent with GSC, *First Contact* has treatment components such as personalized feedback on substance use and exercises that examine the pros and cons of use and alternatives to use. Unlike GSC, the exercises are designed to be completed in-session. Homework was not recommended by our youth advisory committee. *First Contact* has also added an exercise to help clients see their use in the context of other life goals (see exercise for Session 3, **Things That Are Important to Me**) and an exercise to help clients understand the change process (see exercise for Session 4, **Stages of Change**). These clinical materials also differ from materials used with adults in that the materials have been carefully reviewed by young people for appropriate wording and relevance to youth.

Stages of Change

The development of *First Contact* was also influenced by Prochaska and Diclemente's Transtheoretical Model (Prochaska, DiClemente & Norcross, 1992). According to this model, people progress through five stages as they try to change their substance use. Prochaska sees the experience gained from previous attempts to quit as the key to eventually changing for good. Although the Stages of Change concept was initially identified and developed in studies of smoking cessation, these stages have also been applied to other types of health behaviours (DiClemente & Hughes, 1990).

The five Stages of Change are precontemplation, contemplation, preparation, action, and maintenance.

1. **Precontemplation** refers to the stage in which people do not intend to make any changes in their use. According to survey studies of the general population, many people spend years in this stage (Prochaska et al., 1992).
2. In the **Contemplation** stage, a person starts to recognize the costs in addition to the benefits of drug use and begins to consider the idea of change.
3. Some people then progress to the **Preparation** stage, where they make the decision to change and think about how to make a change.
4. In the **Action** stage, people begin to change their behaviour and actively use and generate strategies to help initiate that change.
5. Once people have succeeded at making and maintaining a change (usually for a period of three to six months), they are considered to have moved into the **Maintenance** stage. If a person does not maintain the change (i.e., has a slip or relapse), he or she may then revert to a previous stage.

In practice, there are several treatment implications of this perspective on change that are incorporated into *First Contact*. A therapist using this model seeks to increase the client's readiness to change by using language and clinical materials in a way that is appropriate to the client's stage (Prochaska et al., 1992). This notion of "working with where the client is at" in terms of readiness to change is echoed in the Motivational Interviewing approach as well (Miller & Rollnick, 1991).

Change is rarely linear; slips and relapses are often part of the change process, leading clients to revert to a reduced willingness to change. The therapist can help clients avoid discouragement by positively reframing the meaning of slips as a learning experience and discussing the Stages of Change concept to provide a longer-term perspective to the change process.

Some clinical exercises can be adjusted to benefit clients across the readiness-to-change continuum. For example, discussing the costs and benefits of change is an important way to address ambivalence to change. However, our clinical experience in groups has shown that young substance users in the preparation and action stages also benefit from a consolidation or elaboration of their reasons for change.

A clinical challenge is the informed risk-taker: a client who presents as unmotivated, but is well aware of his or her behaviour. (These clients are distinct from "precontemplative" youth who are, by definition, unaware of the consequences of their use.) Even with youth who are aware and actively resisting change, however, the therapeutic task is similar. With precontemplative and contemplative clients, one tries to increase perceived risk associated with use in terms of both direct consequences of use (e.g., risk of legal problems) or indirect (e.g., adverse effect on achieving other life goals). Although informed risk-takers may be more resistant to engaging in and discussing the exercises, the Motivational Interviewing approach provides several strategies for dealing with resistance.

THERAPEUTIC STYLE

Similar to other brief motivational interventions, *First Contact*:

- assumes that the client, not the counsellor, is the agent of change. Once clients understand and value the reasons for changing, they have a responsibility to acquire the knowledge and skills to make that change.
- fosters *intrinsic* motivation for change. Although a didactic mode can be appropriate when a client is ready to make a change and requests advice, the therapeutic task when first working with youth is usually to resolve their ambivalence about change. Intrinsic motivation can be undermined when the arguments for change come solely from external sources. The *First Contact* counsellor tries to set up

discussions and experiences where the client voices the consequences of use and a commitment to change. This approach leads to less emphasis on the counsellor's role as a teacher, and facilitates the counsellor's ability to establish a therapeutic alliance, a key issue in the initial stages of therapy.

- tries (even with court-ordered clients) to explicitly and implicitly emphasize how the client is in control of the decision to change. Providing a sense of control, and respect for their goals, is a key to establishing an effective working relationship or therapeutic alliance with clients.

Practical strategies

Even though the goal of enhancing client motivation is vital, often the means to achieve that end are elusive. For advice on how to enhance client motivation, see Miller and Rollnick's (1991) *Motivational Interviewing*, in which they describe five basic principles for motivational interventions:

- **Express empathy** by listening rather than telling.
- **Develop discrepancy** between where clients are, and where they want to be.
- **Avoid argumentation** about substance use and related risks.
- **Roll with resistance** instead of meeting it head-on.
- **Support self-efficacy** by noting and encouraging even the small ways that the clients have tried to change their substance use.

Traditional approaches to treating substance use aim to make clients aware, through education and confrontation, of the problems associated with substance abuse. In contrast, a motivational approach sees the counsellor as someone who assists clients to make decisions about their behaviour and who provides supportive, goal-directed counselling. On a more practical level, counsellors can employ many of the following strategies to achieve these aims:

- eliciting self-motivational statements — a strategy used to help build client motivation by encouraging the client to express a desire to change (for example, the counsellor may try to have the client acknowledge real or potential problems related to use)
- listening with empathy — a response showing that one understands or is seeking to fully understand the client's situation

- using open-ended questions — a method that encourages clients to voice their beliefs and concerns about substance use instead of the counsellor telling the clients how they should feel or what to do
- affirming the client — statements that sincerely compliment clients and reinforce their efforts
- reframing — a strategy where clients are invited to examine their perceptions in a new light
- summarizing — a longer, reflective statement of what the client has said during a session.

A detailed discussion of the use of these and other Motivational Interviewing strategies is found in Miller and Rollnick's *Motivational Interviewing* (1991) and Motivational Interviewing Video series (1998), and in *Motivational Strategies for Promoting Self-Change* (ARF, 1995).

Treatment sessions

About the clinical materials

The clinical materials used in *First Contact* consist of three types: session checklists, handouts and progress notes.

The session checklists are for the counsellors and summarize the key topics to cover in each session. Session checklists give the order in which in-session exercises are usually completed and include examples of how to introduce, explain and encourage discussion of each of the exercises.

The handouts include clinical exercises and handouts used by clients. All clinical exercises take only a few minutes to complete so they can be filled out by the client in each session and do not need to be given as homework assignments between sessions.

The progress notes list the key topics that are covered in each session. The notes also provide a standardized method for reporting on clients' substance use during the week and substance use goals. Additional space is also provided for other issues that are specific to the particular client. For example, the additional space in the first progress note can be used to note the specific pros and cons about drug use that the client mentioned during the **Decision to Change** exercise.

The progress notes included in this manual are examples of how to document each session. They may need to be adapted for use in your setting.

Giving personalized
feedback at assessment

Giving personalized feedback at assessment

Materials needed

Counsellor's materials
1. Goals for Giving Personalized Feedback at Assessment
2. Checklist for Giving Personalized Feedback at Assessment

Client handouts
1. Facts About *First Contact*
2. Information at Assessment (five pages)
   a. Alcohol — The Big Picture
   b. Cannabis (Hash, Weed, Pot) — The Big Picture
   c. Cocaine (Crack) — The Big Picture
   d. Hallucinogens (LSD, Acid) — The Big Picture
   e. Stimulants (Amphetamines, Speed) —
      The Big Picture

Each treatment setting has specific constraints and requirements in terms of assessment and feedback. For information on how to complete an assessment for substance use, see *Youth and Drugs: An Education Package for Professionals* (ARF, 1991), which suggests that an assessment should examine:

- the nature and severity of drug use
- the nature and severity of problems in other life areas
- readiness for change
- reasons for seeking treatment
- previous treatment experiences
- previous quit attempts
- social and environmental support
- mental and physical health
- family relations
- school adjustment
- peer relationships.

Assessment not only functions as a means to determine a client's appropriateness for *First Contact* (e.g., no urgent medical or psychiatric issues), but it is also an opportunity to engage the client in the therapy process. The *First Contact* materials for feedback at assessment are intended to give the clinician additional opportunities to engage and inform the client. However, even collecting general information such as a history of quit attempts can be done in a way that incorporates Motivational Interviewing strategies.

For example, during the evaluation follow-up of *First Contact* clients at the Centre for Addiction and Mental Health (CAMH), youth consistently reported that one of the most helpful and memorable aspects of their assessment experience was completing a drug use history questionnaire, an instrument that asks details about substance use. Particularly striking to clients was the number of days in the past 90 days that they had used a particular substance; this number was usually greater than they had expected.

PERSONALIZED FEEDBACK ON SUBSTANCE USE AND CONSEQUENCES

Providing personalized feedback on substance use to clients at assessment serves two distinct purposes. First, it incorporates information on substance use in the general population of youth and provides a normative standard for clients to compare their use. Normative information serves as a way of correcting client misconceptions such as "everyone uses." This allows for the development of discrepancy, which is believed to increase motivation (Miller & Rollnick, 1991). Second, even for those who do drop out of treatment, this type of feedback can help them contemplate future change. The video series by Miller and colleagues includes a training tape devoted to showing how to provide normative feedback on use and consequences in a Motivational Interviewing style (Miller & Rollnick, 1998).

To aid in comparing clients' use to normative data, the counsellor should collect information on the quantity and frequency of use for the five types of drugs for which *First Contact* provides survey data.

Discussing the client's drug use in comparison with survey data is the next step, thereby increasing the relevance of this feedback. The normative data used in *First Contact* are from young people (15 to 24 years of age) and include alcohol, cannabis, cocaine, stimulants and hallucinogens. These data are from the 1994 *Canada's Alcohol and Other Drugs Survey*. In addition, data on the relationship between frequency of use and likelihood of negative consequences are provided, from the 1990 *Ontario Health Survey*.

During the field testing and piloting of *First Contact,* both clinicians and clients felt that it was important to make available general information on drug effects. As part of the assessment interview, the "Do you know..." series of drug information pamphlets, developed and produced by CAMH, are made available to youth. These pamphlets include information on physical and psychological effects of drug use, health risk, short-term and long-term consequences of use. For information or to order these pamphlets, call CAMH marketing (1-800-661-1111). These pamphlets should be made available throughout the treatment program.

Facts about *First Contact* is an example of the handout that was given to clients to describe the program. This handout can be modified to suit the program as you have adapted it to your setting.

Goals
for giving personalized feedback at assessment

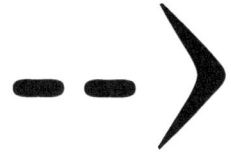

$--\rangle$

1 Following completion of the assessment, increase the client's interest in participating in treatment by:
  a. eliciting reasons for change from the client
  b. presenting normative information on youth substance use and consequences of use
  c. making drug education pamphlets available
  d. clearly describing the purpose and format of the *First Contact* program.

2 Discuss and address barriers to attending the program.

Checklist
for giving personalized feedback at assessment

☑

Guidelines for the counsellor	Tips on what to do with or say to the client
☐ 1. Give normative information and other summary information gathered at assessment. Review the **Information at Assessment** handouts.	"This pie chart shows you how many people aged 15 to 24 reported using... [e.g., cannabis]. This information came from a national survey done in 1994. The bar graph shows the relationship between use and reported negative consequences." To personalize this information, ask: • What do you think about this? • Does this make sense to you? If not, why not? • Does this information surprise you?
☐ 2. Offer the drug education pamphlets.	"Some people may want more information on the effects, for example, physical effects, about the drugs they use. If you are interested in taking any of these pamphlets to read more, please help yourself." Youth may be uncomfortable taking them in front of the counsellor; you may want to have the pamphlets available in a waiting area or outside the counsellor's office.

Guidelines for the counsellor	Tips on what to do with or say to the client
❑ 3. Introduce *First Contact* if appropriate. (See **Who is the *First Contact* program appropriate for?** on page 3.)	
❑ a. Describe the purpose of *First Contact*.	"People have different ideas about what treatment is about. Let me tell you something about this program..." [see **Facts About *First Contact*: What is the program about?** for the points that can be discussed.]
❑ b. Describe how *First Contact* works.	"This program is really to help you look at the impact of your use on your life. To help with that the program includes..." [see **Facts About *First Contact*: How does it work?** for the points that can be mentioned.]
❑ c. Describe who comes to *First Contact*. (This is especially important when providing *First Contact* in a group format.)	"You might also be wondering what the people who come to this program are like. While everybody has their own unique situation, here are some of the things we know about the people who come here..." [see **Facts About *First Contact*: Who comes?** for examples of the information that can be provided. This summary information represents information for the clients seeking treatment at the Centre for Addiction and Mental Health. This kind of summary information should be obtained for each treatment setting.]
❑ 4. Examine barriers to treatment.	"What would stop you from coming to the group on May 15?"
❑ 5. Introduce individual counsellor or group facilitator (if not the same person as the assessor) and give phone number and appointments.	

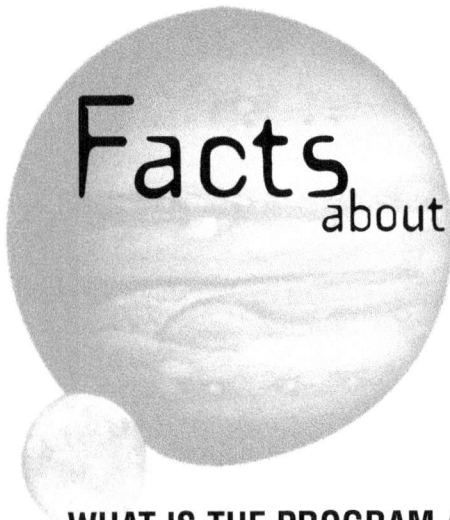

Facts about *First Contact*

WHAT IS THE PROGRAM ABOUT?

First Contact:

- is for young people who are willing to look at the impact of their alcohol and/or drug use on their lives
- helps youth understand that they are not alone: others are dealing with some of the same concerns
- offers treatment in an accepting atmosphere
- encourages youth to make their own choices and decisions about their lives
- is based on the belief that the first few appointments are important in getting the change process started
- can refer you to additional treatment and follow-up.

HOW DOES IT WORK?

- You will meet with a counsellor to help get a picture of your current situation.
- You will look at the pros and cons of your alcohol or drug use and decide what changes you want to make.
- You will be actively involved in setting your own goals.
- You will identify risky drinking or drug use situations and develop alternate ways of dealing with them.
- (group only) Members receive encouragement and suggestions from other youth dealing with many of the same issues.
- (group only) How much you participate is up to you. You will not be "put on the spot."
- Please arrive alcohol- and drug-free for your weekly sessions.

WHO COMES?

Seventy per cent of the youth attending say this is their first time coming for help.

Age:
- The youth attending the program are between the ages of 14 and 23.
- To date, two-thirds are between the ages of 16 and 20.

When asked about their primary concerns:
- 37 per cent say cannabis (hash, pot)
- 26 per cent say alcohol
- 10 per cent say cocaine (crack)
- 10 per cent say stimulants (speed, ice)
- 4 per cent say hallucinogens (LSD, ecstasy).

REASONS FOR COMING TO THE PROGRAM:

- one-third came in because of their own concerns
- one-third came in because friends and family are concerned
- one-third came in for other reasons (e.g., other social service or health care professional).

You have an appointment with _____
on _____ at _____
If for any reason you cannot keep your appointment, please call.

Alcohol
The Big Picture

Alcohol use among
Canadian youth (15 – 24 yrs)

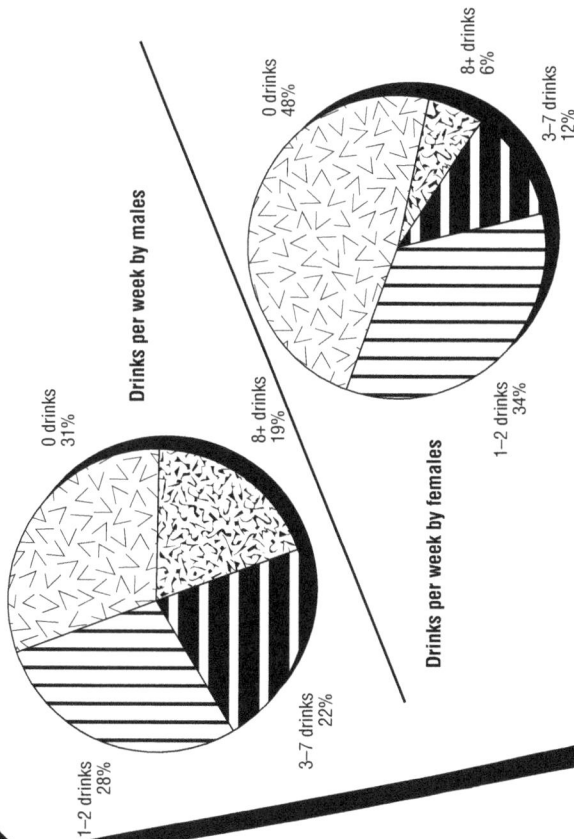

Drinks per week by males

0 drinks
48%

8+ drinks
6%

3–7 drinks
12%

1–2 drinks
34%

Drinks per week by females

0 drinks
31%

8+ drinks
19%

3–7 drinks
22%

1–2 drinks
28%

The more you drink
the more problems you'll have

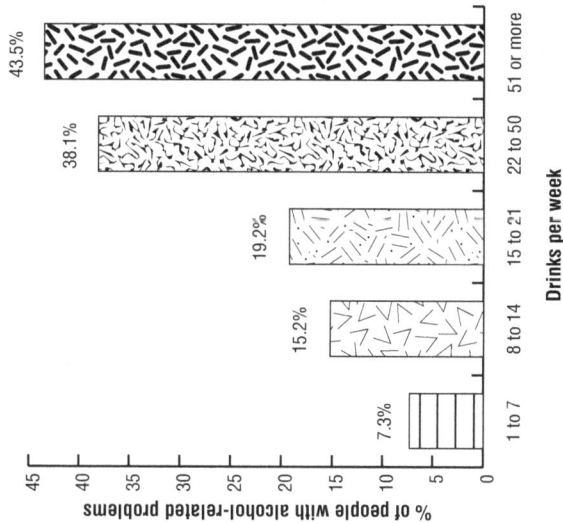

% of people with alcohol-related problems

7.3%
15.2%
19.2%
38.1%
43.5%

| 1 to 7 | 8 to 14 | 15 to 21 | 22 to 50 | 51 or more |

Drinks per week

How does your drinking compare?

Next to caffeine, alcohol is the most widely used drug. Alcohol is a depressant. If abused, it can impair your ability to think, to make decisions and to function in day-to-day life.

The pie charts above show what more than 1,800 Canadians aged 15 to 24 said about how much they drink.

How likely are you to have problems?

A 1994 survey of more than 12,000 people asked how alcohol use affected their:
- physical health
- outlook on life
- relationships with family and friends
- finances
- work or school.

The results showed that the more alcohol people drank in a week, the greater the chance that it was causing problems in one or more of these areas. Look at the chart above and see where you fit.

Cannabis (Hash, Weed, Pot)
The Big Picture

Cannabis use among Canadian youth (15 – 24 yrs)

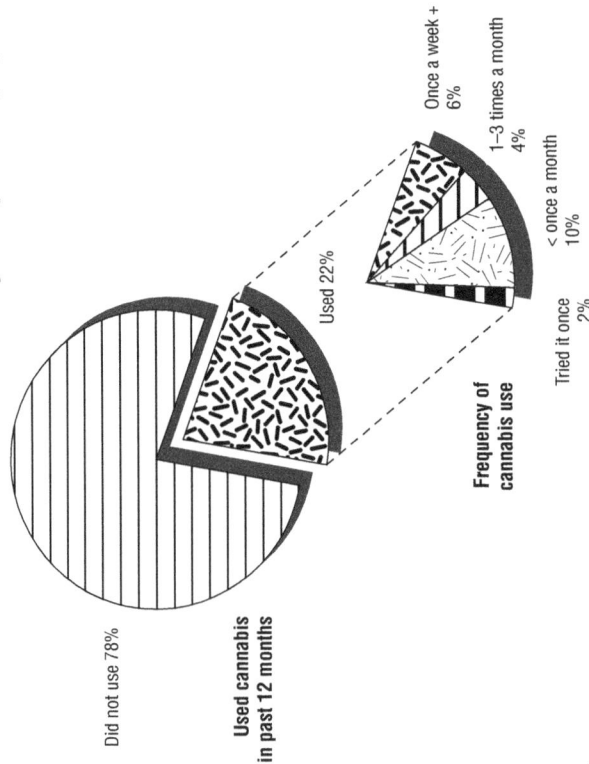

Did not use 78%

Used cannabis in past 12 months

Used 22%

Tried it once 2%

< once a month 10%

1–3 times a month 4%

Once a week + 6%

Frequency of cannabis use

How does your use compare?

Cannabis is the most widely used illegal drug in Canada. In a 1994 survey of more than 1,800 Canadians aged 15 to 24, 22% said that they have used marijuana or other forms of cannabis once or more in their lives. The other pie slice shows how often these young Canadians used cannabis.

The more you use the more problems you'll have

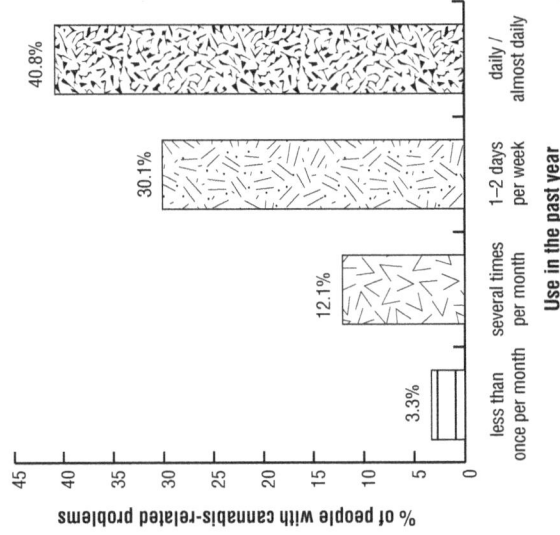

% of people with cannabis-related problems

- 3.3% — less than once per month
- 12.1% — several times per month
- 30.1% — 1–2 days per week
- 40.8% — daily / almost daily

Use in the past year

How likely are you to have problems?

A 1991 survey of more than 9,000 people asked how cannabis use affected their:
- physical health
- outlook on life
- relationships with family and friends
- finances
- work or school.

The results showed that the more cannabis people used in the last year, the greater the chance that it was causing problems in one or more of these areas. Look at the chart above and see where you fit.

Cocaine (Crack) The Big Picture

Cocaine use among
Canadian youth (15 – 24 yrs)

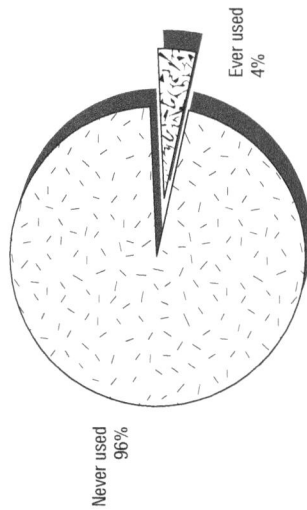

Never used
96%

Ever used
4%

The more you use
the more problems you'll have

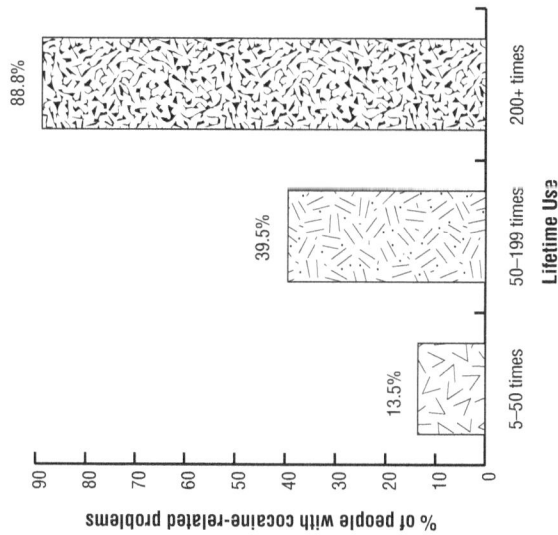

% of people with cocaine-related problems

	13.5%	39.5%	88.8%
	5-50 times	50-199 times	200+ times

Lifetime Use

How does your use compare?

In a 1994 survey of more than 1,800 Canadians aged 15 to 24, about 4% said that they had used cocaine or crack at least once in their lives.

How likely are you to have problems?

A 1991 survey of more than 9,000 people asked how cocaine use affected their:

- physical health
- outlook on life
- relationships with family and friends
- finances
- work or school.

The results showed that the more cocaine people used, the greater the chance that it was causing problems in one or more of these areas. Look at the chart above and see where you fit.

Hallucinogens (LSD, Acid) — The Big Picture

Hallucinogen use among Canadian youth (15 – 24 yrs)

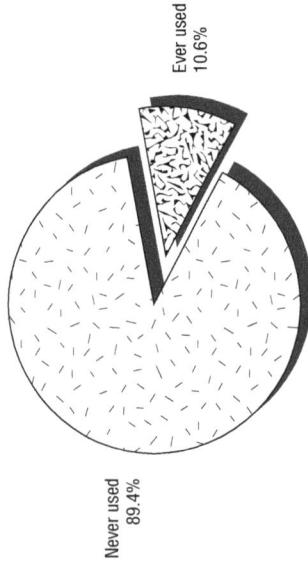

Ever used
10.6%

Never used
89.4%

The more you use the more problems you'll have

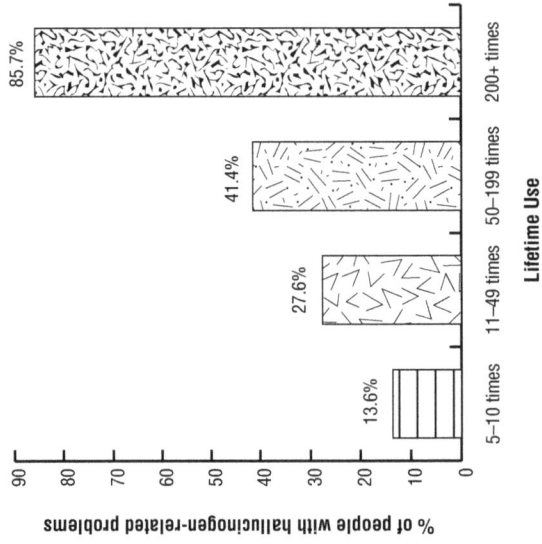

% of people with hallucinogen-related problems

Lifetime Use	%
5–10 times	13.6%
11–49 times	27.6%
50–199 times	41.4%
200+ times	85.7%

Lifetime Use

How does your use compare?

In a 1994 survey of more than 1,800 Canadians aged 15 to 24, about 11 per cent said that they had used hallucinogens such as LSD at least once in their lives.

How likely are you to have problems?

A 1991 survey of more than 9,000 people asked how hallucinogen use affected their:

- physical health
- outlook on life
- relationships with family and friends
- finances
- work or school.

The results showed that the more hallucinogens people used, the greater the chance that it was causing problems in one or more of these areas. Look at the chart above and see where you fit.

Stimulants (Amphetamines, Speed) The Big Picture

Stimulant use among Canadian youth (15 – 24 yrs)

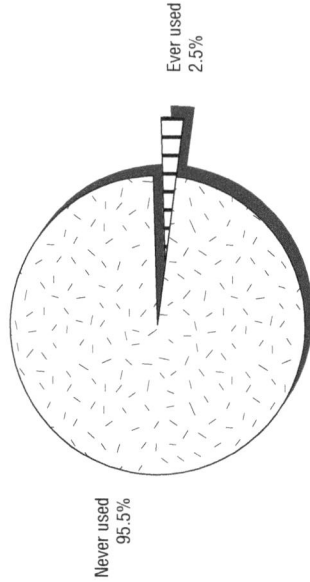

Never used 95.5%

Ever used 2.5%

The more you use the more problems you'll have

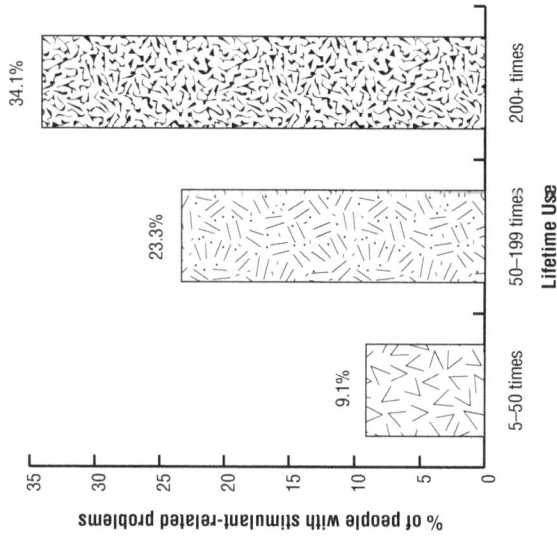

% of people with stimulant-related problems

9.1% — 5–50 times
23.3% — 50–199 times
34.1% — 200+ times

Lifetime Use

How does your use compare?

In a 1994 survey of more than 1,800 Canadians aged 15 to 24, about 2.5 per cent said that they had used stimulants such as speed at least once in their lives.

How likely are you to have problems?

A 1991 survey of more than 9,000 people asked how stimulant use affected their:

- physical health
- outlook on life
- relationships with family and friends
- finances
- work or school

The results showed that the more stimulants people used, the greater the chance that it was causing problems in one or more of these areas. Look at the chart above and see where you fit.

Session 1
Decision to change

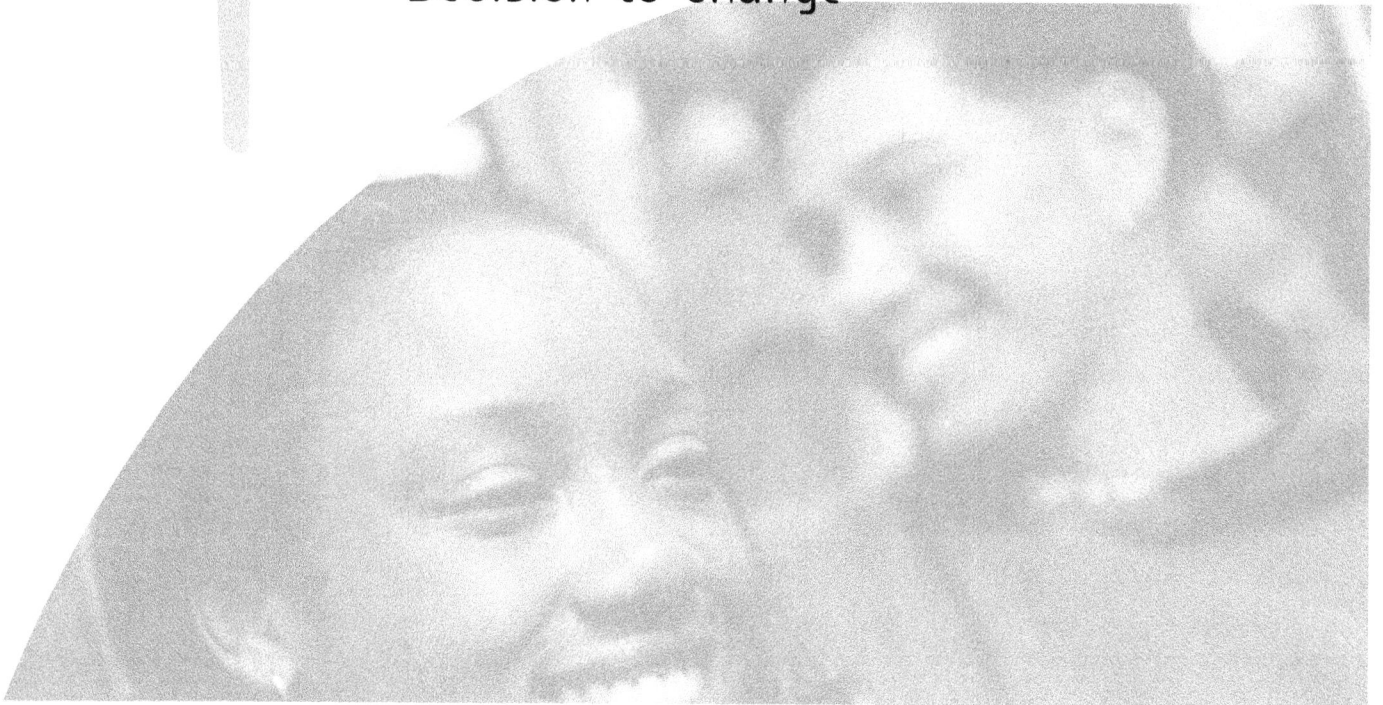

Session 1
Decision
to change

Materials needed

Counsellor's materials
1. Goals for Session 1: Decision to Change
2. Checklist for Session 1: Decision to Change
3. Progress Note for Session 1: Decision to Change

Client handouts
1. Decision to Change
2. Check-in

An important part of beginning therapy and reducing clients' initial anxiety, whether for group or individual therapy, is to provide a clear understanding of the purpose of the sessions and your role as a counsellor. The purpose of *First Contact* is to help young people look at the impact that their use of drugs and alcohol has had on their lives, to acknowledge that the decision to change is theirs, and to recognize that increased awareness about risks of, and alternatives to, substance use is part of an informed decision.

THE ROLE OF THE COUNSELLOR

Consistent with Motivational Interviewing, the counsellor does not assume the role of teacher, but helps clients explore their substance use issues. In keeping with a Stages-of-Change perspective, the counsellor facilitates the clients' exploration of the costs and benefits of their substance use. This exploration is even useful for clients who are ambivalent about change. As clients' readiness to change increases, the counsellor can then help them explore strategies for change.

BREAKING THE ICE, ESTABLISHING GROUP COHESION AND GROUP RULES

If you are working with groups, Session 1 is a time to facilitate group formation. One of the ways to accomplish this goal is to have clients introduce themselves and ask them to say what brought them to treatment and what they hope to get out of treatment. In developing *First Contact,* we have used and included icebreakers in the Session 1 checklist. An icebreaker is one way to encourage people to disclose some personal information that is not necessarily related to drug use.

During development and field tests, *First Contact* was primarily delivered in a group format. In groups where clients have not met each other before, it is common for clients to be quiet in the first half of Session 1 and only speak when spoken to. To develop group cohesion in such a short period of time can be a daunting task for the counsellor.

We find that normalizing the initial anxiety and providing informal time for clients to get to know one another (e.g., mid-session break during a two-hour group) facilitates the process of establishing group cohesion. Splitting clients into dyads for the client introductions (the ice-breaker exercise) also appears to facilitate the cohesion process. We typically have the clients tell each other their name, age, favourite music or hobby, one way in which they are similar and one way in which they differ. Finally, each person introduces the other member of the dyad to the group. The change from group to dyad and back also provides a short opportunity to move around and do something new in the group.

The Session 1 checklist also provides an opportunity to discuss differences among group members. This discussion helps provide a rationale for group rules: because the group members differ in terms of gender, family background, substance use, etc., group rules can make everyone feel comfortable and make it easier to communicate in a respectful way. At this point, you will review rules around confidentiality, conduct, and coming drug-free and on time to group.

Regarding diversity within groups, we have worked with groups that differ in terms of gender, readiness to change, and cultural/ethnic background. We find that counsellors experienced with group work can overcome the potential obstacles that group diversity can present (Schulman, 1999). When special needs emerge, having case management sessions or individual therapy to supplement the group work can help address these needs.

DECISION TO CHANGE

The **Decision to Change** exercise provides a way to discuss and address clients' ambivalence to change. Based on the original work by Jannis and Mann (1977), the **Decision to Change** exercise asks clients to identify the pros and cons of changing and the pros and cons of using. The primary goal of this exercise is to increase clients' awareness of changing use as a decision where some trade-offs are made. Just being aware of the possible pros and cons, and asking clients to prioritize them, facilitates self re-evaluation, a change process that, according to Prochaska and DiClemente (1992), is crucial to increasing one's readiness to change. The **Decision to Change** exercise gives clients a way to talk about the difficulties of changing as well as the consequences of not changing.

While a counsellor may have the urge to talk about how to solve the problems or overcome the obstacles presented, it is important first to acknowledge the obstacles and what would be lost by changing. In a group, members will talk about their own experiences with an obstacle to change. You will need to use some clinical judgment in situations where a client seems to be getting discouraged by the obstacles to change. To help a client gain perspective on the obstacles to change, provide (or have the group provide) some encouraging words and support self-efficacy. For example, it is sometimes useful to affirm a client's decision to seek help, or to draw parallels between a previous accomplishment that took time and effort, and his or her present situation. In this way, the counsellor highlights the client's resources for change without taking on the teacher role.

Finally, although the **Check-in** exercise will be completed in Session 2, it is worthwhile to introduce this exercise at the end of the first session. Previewing the **Check-in** exercise gets clients thinking about monitoring use, urges, and coping during the coming week so that this information will not be as difficult to recall in Session 2.

GOAL SETTING

The *First Contact* program is relevant both for people with non-abstinent goals and for those who are prepared to quit altogether. Early in the treatment process, one should clarify clients' substance use goals, particularly their intentions about stopping or reducing their use. Many clients may not choose a goal of abstinence. *First Contact* takes a pragmatic approach by assisting clients to establish and work towards their substance use goals. In the short term, this strategy seeks to decrease the adverse impact of substance use in a style that supports clients' autonomy. In the long term, setting and reviewing use goals can be a process whereby clients build the motivation and skills needed for minimal or no use. Research supports the notion of providing goal choice in that:

- There appears to be no basis for expecting that the therapist assigning treatment goals to clients will affect outcome (Sanchez-Craig, Annis, Bornet & MacDonald, 1984).
- Clients will be more likely to comply with treatment when they themselves have made the decision to pursue that strategy (Sobell & Sobell, 1993).

In discussing substance-use goals, it is important to make clear to the client that allowing goal choice does not mean that the counsellor is condoning or encouraging substance use; in particular, the use of alcohol by anyone who is under legal drinking age and the use of illicit substances by youth of any age. In the spirit of informed choices, this point can be made by stating that the most effective way to eliminate the chance of negative substance-related consequences is to *not use at all.* For those clients who do not choose a goal of abstinence, however, it is important to provide the message that reduction can decrease substance-use-related harms.

When clients consider reducing their use, the counsellor should emphasize the feasibility and reasonableness of the chosen goal. For example, when there are reasons why substance use would be too great a risk (e.g., if it would lead to serious legal problems or loss of family relationships), this would be an opportunity for the counsellor to determine how the client perceives the potential risks involved, even with reduced use, and the benefits of an abstinence goal.

Because most clients will not know what goal is most realistic for them at first, weekly review of clients' goals is recommended. A reduced substance-use goal should be clearly defined so that:

- The client has specific, well-thought-out rules about drinking or drug use limits when he or she encounters a possible high-risk situation.
- The substance use goal does not change over time in a way that leads to the pretreatment substance use pattern.

Goals for Session 1: Decision to change ‑ ‑ >

1 Provide a clear understanding of the purpose, format and goals of *First Contact*.

2 Facilitate group formation by:
- a. introducing group leaders and clients
- b. establishing group rules, norms, and expectations
- c. beginning to highlight commonalities among group members to foster support.

3 Create a comfortable, accepting atmosphere.

4 Encourage discussion of what brought them here and what they hope to get out of treatment.

5 Complete the **Decision to Change** exercise. Goals:
- a. Help client to become aware of decision process.
- b. Provide a forum to talk about the difficulties of changing.
- c. Highlight the consequences of changing and not changing.
- d. Acknowledge what would be lost by changing.
- e. Introduce the idea of choice and control with regard to drug use.

6 Introduce weekly use/goal monitoring **(Check-in)**.

Checklist
for Session 1: Decision to change

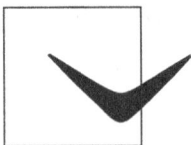

Guidelines for the counsellor	Tips on what to do with or say to the client
☐ 1. Introduce the program.	"This group is for people aged 14 to 20 and you will be meeting for two hours, once a week for four weeks. After four weeks, this group will end, and you can decide where you want to go from there."
	"The purpose of the group is to look at the impact that drugs and alcohol have had on your lives. This is your group and you are here to help each other out; therefore what you have to say to each other is very important. We (the therapists) are here to help build some trust and encourage you to participate. We also have some problem-solving tools to share with you."
	"Some of you are in different places when it comes to your drug use: • Some of you have no intention of changing your drug use, and are here because you feel you have no other choice. • Some of you have very mixed feelings about changing your drug use. • Some of you are thinking about changes, but don't know where to start. • Some of you have already made some changes."
☐ 2. Discuss participation in group and confidentiality.	"This group is a place where you can start solving some of the problems you're facing. So, the more you share, the more you are going to get out of the group. We will have a chance in the group to talk about your life goals and your drug use goals, but what you actually decide to do is up to you. Because people are going to be sharing things, it is important that we all agree that what is said in the group stays in the group."
	"Something that is important for us to talk about is your confidentiality. What is said in here stays in this room. We need your permission to talk to or release information to others. However, there are some limits to confidentiality. If you are going to harm yourself or others or if child abuse is an issue, then legally we need to break confidentiality. But aside from those exceptions, your confidentiality is maintained."

Guidelines for the counsellor	Tips on what to do with or say to the client
☐ 3. Introduce clients.	"In this group, we are going to be talking a lot and getting to know one another better. As a way of starting this…" Ice breaker 1: "To find out more about each other, I would like you to split up into pairs and discuss the following things with your partners: • How old are they? • What is their favourite music or hobby? • What is one way that you are alike? • What is one way that you are different? After you talk about these, each one of you will tell us about your partner." Ice breaker 2: "If you had $50 to spend, what… CD would you buy? movie would you go to? place would you go to dinner or dancing? hobby would you spend it on?"
☐ 4. Tune into differences and group rules.	Differences exercise (done on a flipchart or blackboard): "We're going to ask you to talk about some of the ways people in this group might differ from one another [give an example such as sex, background, substance of use]. What might be some ways we can make everyone feel comfortable in this group despite these differences? What should the rules of the group be?" Note: Be sure that the following are included if they don't come up in discussion: • confidentiality (both agency policy and confidentiality between members) • general rules of conduct (e.g., listening and not putting down) • coming straight and coming on time.
☐ 5. Explore clients' concerns.	"Some of you may have been anxious about this first group meeting and wondered what would happen. I can tell you that my co-therapist and I have led many of these groups, and you'll be surprised at how quickly we get to know each other, and how people really help each other out." "What does it feel like to: • be forced to come here? • be expected to talk? • be told that you have a problem? • be told by others to quit using? • wonder whether you are going to connect with other group members?"

Guidelines for the counsellor	Tips on what to do with or say to the client
❑ 6. Discuss **Decision to Change** exercise.	"We'd like to talk about some of the issues you may be struggling with in deciding to stop or reduce your use. What will you gain — and lose — by changing? What about not changing?" Ways of discussing exercise: "Which cost (or benefit) is most important?" "Why are you concerned about that cost?" "How mixed are your feelings about changing your use?" "What are some of the fears or hopes you have right now?"
❑ 7. Introduce **Check-in** exercise.	"This sheet is what we will be using each week as a way of you telling the group what went well during the week and what did not go well. Over the next week, think about what your drug use goal will be. Also over the next week, try to remember when you used, when you craved and how you dealt with it. Those are the things that we will talk about next week."
❑ 8. Wrap up.	"What's one thing you will do this week towards your substance use goal?" "Was the group what you expected? Do you have any questions?" "What will you be saying to each other on the way back to the elevator? It is important to say it here in the group." "What stood out for you in this session? What would you say to someone else about today's group?"

Progress Note for Session 1: Decision to change

• • • • • •

NAME: _____   FILE#: _____   SESSION DATE: _____

❑ Client Cancelled (specify action plan)   Action Plan: _____
❑ No Show (specify action plan)   _____
❑ Clinician Cancelled (specify action plan) _____

❑ Attended Session 1 of the *First Contact* program. This motivational treatment program is designed
   to help youth look at the impact alcohol and other drugs has had on their lives.

This session was conducted in the following format: ❑ Individual   ❑ Group

This session covered the following (check one box):

Covered	Not Covered	
❑	❑	The program was introduced by the counsellor(s).
❑	❑	Information about participating in the program and confidentiality was reviewed.
❑	❑	Client introductions were made and an ice-breaker exercise was completed.
❑	❑	Differences in the group were examined and group rules were reviewed.
❑	❑	Client concerns about being involved in treatment were discussed.
❑	❑	Completed and discussed the **Decision to Change** exercise. (That is, weighing the costs and benefits of stopping or reducing use of drugs)
❑	❑	In preparation for session 2, introduced **Check-in.**
❑	❑	Asked client(s) to take one step over the next week towards their drug use goal and reviewed today's group experience.

Substance Use Since Last Session: ❑ Abstinent   ❑ Non-Abstinent
Substances/Frequency/Quantity: _____
Drug Use Goal(s):
Participation in Group: ❑ Low   ❑ Moderate   ❑ High
Therapists at this session were (for group only):
Outcome of Session:
❑ Next Session Scheduled for: _____
❑ Treatment Terminated (client initiated)*
❑ Treatment Terminated (clinician initiated)*   *discharge summary req'd
Additional Notes:

_____   _____
Signature/Credentials   Date

Decision to change

▬ ▬ ▬ ▬ ▬

In making a decision to change, it can be helpful to think about the **good things** and the **not-so-good things** about using now. Check the top two items that apply to you. Remember, drug use includes drinking.

The good things about using

☐ I don't have to deal with my problems
☐ I feel more confident
☐ I have something to do when I am bored
☐ I fit in with my friends
☐ I have more fun at parties
☐ It helps me calm down and relax

List any others

The not-so-good things about using

☐ I feel guilty or ashamed
☐ I don't like the way I look and feel
  after use
☐ It is a source of conflict between me and
  my family
☐ It is a source of conflict between me and
  my friends
☐ I will have money problems
☐ I will continue to feel anxious and
  depressed
☐ I will harm my health

List any others

It is also helpful to think about the **good things** and **not-so-good things** about reducing or stopping your drug use. Check the top two items that apply to you. Remember, drug use includes drinking.

Not-so-good things about reducing or stopping my use

❑ I will feel more depressed and/or anxious
❑ I won't have anything to do when I'm bored
❑ I won't have any way to relax
❑ I will have to rearrange my social life
❑ I won't "fit in" with some friends
❑ I don't know if I can make change stick

List any others

Good things about reducing or stopping my use

❑ I will feel more in control over my life
❑ I will gain more self-esteem
❑ It will improve my relationship with my family
❑ I will have more money
❑ I will have fewer problems at work or school
❑ It will make it easier to achieve life goals

List any others

Adapted from Janis & Mann (1977).

Check-in

I USED OR THOUGHT ABOUT USING ON...

I WANTED TO USE...

Monday

Tuesday

Wednesday

Thursday

Friday

Saturday

Sunday

☐ When I felt the need to cope

☐ When I just wanted to have fun

☐ Out of habit

☐ Other

My goals for the next week are:

☐ Not to use

☐ Reduced use

☐ Work on one of my life goals

☐ Other

☐ Used

☐ Did something else

☐ Thought about consequences

☐ Avoided using

☐ Other

MY GOALS

WHEN I THOUGHT ABOUT USING, I...

My week was

0	5	10
lousy	OK	fantastic

Session

2
Triggers, consequences and alternatives

Session 2
Triggers, consequences and alternatives

Materials needed

Counsellors materials
1. Goals for Session 2: Triggers, Consequences and Alternatives
2. Checklist for Session 2: Triggers, Consequences and Alternatives
3. Progress Note for Session 2: Triggers, Consequences and Alternatives

Client handouts
1. Check-in
2. Triggers, Consequences and Alternatives

Many of the themes introduced in Session 1 are continued in Session 2. For example, clients will continue to talk about the costs and benefits of change they have experienced or expect to experience. When conducting *First Contact* in a group format, acknowledging and normalizing the client's difficulties and seeing whether other group members have had similar experiences provides support for the client and builds group cohesion.

CHECK-IN

The **Check-in** exercise is a way to reinforce and elaborate on themes introduced in Session 1. Part of the **Check-in** asks clients to recall their use and/or urges to use substances during the past week. This allows clients to increase their awareness of the situations where they use or have urges to use, and allows the counsellor to highlight any successes, even if they are simply reducing the quantity or frequency of use. The counsellor should explore incidents of success carefully, to ensure that clients understand how they actually succeeded. Many young clients simply report that they did not use and need prompting to clarify which skills, strategies, or alternatives they used to succeed.

Other parts of the **Check-in** allow for discussion of triggers to use, alternatives to use, and drug use goals. One activity that counsellors have used to increase the extent to which clients talk with one another is to have clients check in with each other. That is, clients complete the exercise as they normally would and then the person next to them asks them two questions about their **Check-in** sheet.

EXPLORING PATTERNS OF USE

The **Triggers, Consequences and Alternatives** exercise can help clients understand their use patterns by emphasizing the link between the triggers/antecedents of use and the resulting positive and negative consequences. Many of the goals of this exercise are drawn from issues raised during the check-in, such as how to identify triggers and generating alternatives to use. Sometimes clients maintain that there are no triggers to their use. What usually helps in this situation is to go over the potential list of people, places, and things (e.g., emotions, time of day) that can serve as triggers. Also, clients may have mentioned something during the **Check-in** exercise that provides clues as to what triggers are salient to them.

It is important to talk about the timing of the consequences of use if the subject does not naturally come up in discussion. On one hand, when people drink or use drugs they are seeking the positive consequences (e.g., temporary relaxation) that can occur during or shortly after use. On the other hand, the negative or harmful consequences are often delayed and are difficult to link with the actual substance use. For instance, a gradual decline in the quality of one's schoolwork could be a long-term result of substance use, which would not be directly related to any single occasion of use.

STRATEGIES FOR CHANGE

After discussing the clients' triggers and alternatives to substance use, the counsellor encourages them to select one alternative that they are willing to try during the coming week. Sometimes clients do not feel confident about engaging in new activities in high-risk situations and these concerns need to be explored. Two strategies that are useful in increasing self-efficacy for trying alternatives are:

- identifying what clients are already doing to reduce their use. Clients sometimes fail to realize that they already engage in some activities that deal with urges or remove them from high-risk situations. Even simple things like keeping busy, listening to music, or spending time with family or non-drug-using friends should be acknowledged and encouraged.

- drawing parallels with a previous accomplishment (i.e., "mining" the past). It is also helpful to find out if clients have tried to reduce or quit in the past and find out how they did so. Even if their strategies were only temporarily successful, discussing how those strategies can be modified or supplemented can be a fruitful way to build on the clients' existing resources.

Goals
for Session 2: Triggers, consequences and alternatives

‒ ‒ >

1 Continue to clarify treatment/use goals.

2 Continue to promote idea of choice and control with respect to use.

3 Continue to provide a comfortable/supportive forum to discuss the difficulties and rewards of changing.

4 For groups, continue to highlight commonalities and build group cohesion.

5 Complete the weekly **Check-in** sheet.
Goals:
   a. Monitor progress.
   b. Highlight successes.
   c. Aid in goal-setting (i.e., drug use and life goals).
   d. Increase awareness of urges, cravings, and strategies.
   e. Search for exceptions to usual pattern.
   f. Expand on clean time.
   g. Share strategies.
   h. Identify high-risk situations.

6 Complete the **Triggers, Consequences and Alternatives** exercise.
Goals:
   a. Generate clients' options.
   b. Create awareness of triggers and consequences.
   c. Explore barriers to change.
   d. Increase self-efficacy by identifying what clients are already trying.
   e. Identify relevant successes in past (i.e.,"mining the past").
   f. Help clients understand their use patterns.
   g. Emphasize the connection between consequences and triggers.
   h. Address difference between long- and short-term consequences (positive vs. negative).

Checklist
for Session 2: Triggers, consequences and alternatives

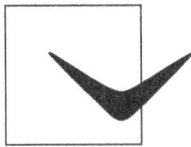

Guidelines for the counsellor	Tips on what to do with or say to the client
☐ 1. Explain the purpose of the **Check-in.**	"This check-in sheet is a way for you to tell the group what went well during the week and what did not go well." Define a craving: A craving can be anything from a thought, such as "I wouldn't mind a joint right now," to a more physical experience, such as palms sweating or difficulty sitting still. Discuss progress over last week: "Tell us about a situation you handled well." "Tell us about your clean time last week ... how can you get more of that?" "Was anything easier/better last week?" Help clients support each other: "What are other peoples' reactions to seeing friends?" "You were nodding when he/she was speaking. What were you thinking about?" Help clients set goals for next week: "What are you going to do more of next week?"
☐ 2. Introduce **Triggers, Consequences and Alternatives** exercise.	"This exercise follows from some of the things that we talked about during the check-in. It will help you to think about the patterns of your use, and what the triggers, payoffs and consequences are. Understanding these connections is the first step to you taking control of your use." Explain triggers, behaviours and consequences — begin by discussing triggers: "When we talk about triggers, we are talking about the situations that lead to use. Triggers can be people, places things, times and feelings. The behaviour is the drug use. The consequences are the things that happen after you use. They can be both positive and negative ... who can give me some examples of triggers?" (Suggestion: have one of the clients at flip chart recording client responses.)

Guidelines for the counsellor	Tips on what to do with or say to the client
	"What triggers happened last week [refer to **Check-in**]?" "What other triggers can you think of?" Discuss consequences: "What is some of the stuff that happens after use? Is there anything you notice about the timing of the consequences?" "Some clients have said that using was really fun in the beginning but that now it is not as much fun. Has anyone experienced that?" "Some consequences are hidden or are lost opportunities. Has anyone experienced something like missing out on something because they were using?" Discuss alternatives to use: "On non-using days, what has worked for you?" "What is going to help you not to use?" "What might be frightening about doing something different when you want to use?" "What would be the easiest thing to do differently?"
❑ 3. Wrap up.	Look at ways that the **Triggers, Consequences and Alternatives** exercise could apply to daily life outside the session: "What is one alternative to use that you can try this week?"

Progress Note
for Session 2:
Triggers, consequences and alternatives

• • • • ● ●

NAME: _____   FILE#: _____   SESSION DATE: _____

❑ Client Cancelled (specify action plan)   Action Plan: _____
❑ No Show (specify action plan)   _____
❑ Clinician Cancelled (specify action plan)   _____

❑ Attended Session 2 of the *First Contact* program.

This session was conducted in the following format: ❑ Individual   ❑ Group

This session covered the following (check one box):

Covered	Not Covered	
❑	❑	The purpose of the **Check-in** was reviewed. Client completed **Check-in.**
❑	❑	Client discussed progress over the last week.
❑	❑	Client was helped by counsellor(s) and group to set goal for next week.
❑	❑	Counsellor(s) introduced **Triggers, Consequences and Alternatives** exercise.
❑	❑	Completed and discussed the **Triggers, Consequences and Alternatives**. That is, examined the triggers and consequences of use.
❑	❑	Explored alternatives to use and asked client(s) to try one alternative to drug use strategy over the next week.
❑	❑	Reviewed today's group experience.

Substance Use Since Last Session: ❑ Abstinent   ❑ Non-Abstinent
Substances/Frequency/Quantity: _____
Drug Use Goal(s):
Participation in Group: ❑ Low ❑ Moderate ❑ High
Therapists at this session were (for group only):
Outcome of Session:
❑ Next Session Scheduled for: _____
❑ Treatment Terminated (client initiated)*
❑ Treatment Terminated (clinician initiated)*   *discharge summary req'd
Additional Notes:

_____   _____
Signature/Credentials   Date

Check-in

Monday

Tuesday

Wednesday

Thursday

Friday

Saturday

Sunday

❑ When I felt the need to cope

❑ When I just wanted to have fun

❑ Out of habit

❑ Other

My goals for the next week are:

❑ Not to use

❑ Reduced use

❑ Work on one of my life goals

❑ Other

❑ Used

❑ Did something else

❑ Thought about consequences

❑ Avoided using

❑ Other

0   5   10

My week was

lousy   OK   fantastic

Triggers,
consequences and alternatives

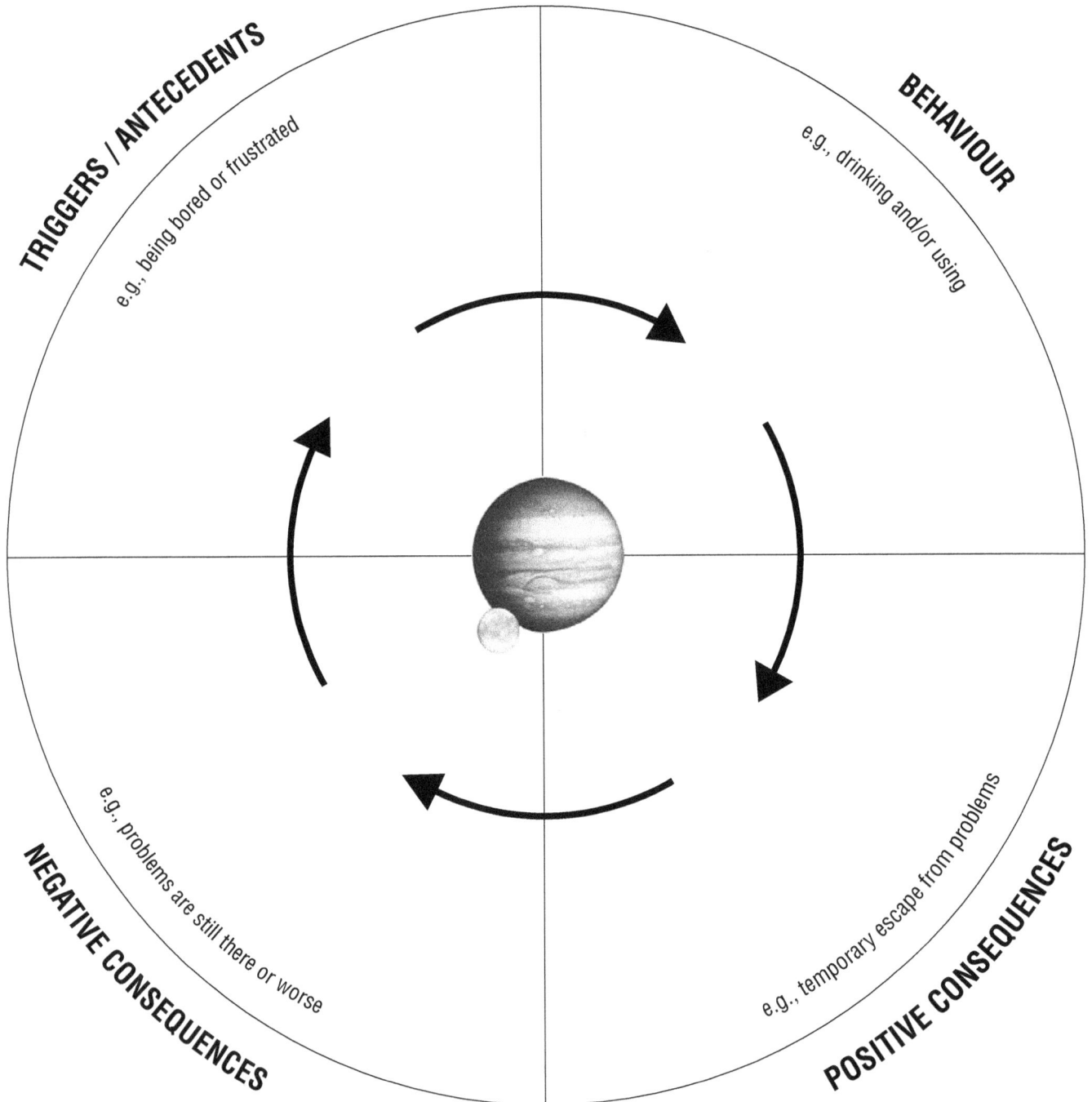

TRIGGERS / ANTECEDENTS
e.g., being bored or frustrated

BEHAVIOUR
e.g., drinking and/or using

NEGATIVE CONSEQUENCES
e.g., problems are still there or worse

POSITIVE CONSEQUENCES
e.g., temporary escape from problems

Session 3

Things that are important to me

Session 3
Things that are
important to me

Materials needed

Counsellor's materials
1. Goals for Session 3: Things That Are Important to Me
2. Checklist for Session 3: Things That Are Important to Me
3. Progress Note for Session 3: Things That Are Important to Me

Client handouts
1. Check-in
2. Things That Are Important to Me

CHECK-IN

Session 3 starts out again with the **Check-in** exercise. The aims of the **Check-in** exercise are reviewed on page 39. Although asking about triggers and alternatives to use is always an integral part of this exercise, a counsellor can probe these issues in more detail based on what was discussed on page 41 in the **Triggers, Consequences and Alternatives** exercise during Session 2.

LIFE GOALS AND VALUES

Session 3 includes the **Things That Are Important to Me** exercise, which relates to the clients' life goals and values. This client handout was adapted from research by Miller and C'deBaca (1994) on goals and values. Several therapeutic approaches, such as solution-focused and motivational interviewing, support the usefulness of exploring life goals and values (Berg, 1995). Clarifying what life goals a client wants to achieve and assessing where he or she is now helps develop discrepancy, one of the key elements of Motivational Interviewing (Miller & Rollnick, 1991). Discussing the things that are important to them helps clients acknowledge their aspirations, strengths, and competencies, rather than focusing exclusively on problematic areas of their lives, reflecting a solution-focused perspective (Berg, 1995).

Understanding clients' life goals also allows for a discussion of how use affects progress towards such goals. Clients may think that drug use helps them to reach some goals, such as being popular. However, most clients will acknowledge that alcohol and other drug use impairs their ability to achieve life goals to some degree (e.g., completing school).

The **Things That Are Important to Me** exercise should also include a discussion of what concrete steps clients can take to start progressing towards their goals. The "Top Ten Ways of Achieving Your Goals" is included in this exercise to help the client decide what the next steps to achieving a goal would be. However, it is important for the counsellor to help in translating the life goals into concrete steps or activities for the client to work on, ideally within the next week. Counsellors can assist in this part of the exercise by helping clients select short-term goals that are realistic and measurable.

Goals
for Session 3: Things that are important to me - - >

1 Reassess treatment/use goals.

2 Find out whether clients tried any new alternative responses since last session.

3 Continue to explore the connection between consequences and triggers.

4 For groups, continue to highlight commonalities and build group cohesion.

5 Complete the **Things That Are Important to Me** exercise.
Goals:
- a. Help clients talk about the future
  (i.e., hopes and expectations).
- b. Create discrepancy.
- c. Explore the role of use in achieving goals.
- d. Review goal achievement:
  - status six months ago
  - current status
  - anticipated progress in six months.
- e. Try to determine plans and next step to achieve goals.

Checklist
for Session 3: Things that are important to me

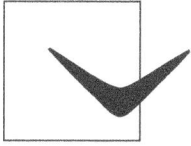

Guidelines for the counsellor	Tips on what to do with or say to the client
☐ 1. **Check-in.**	Discuss progress over the past week: For tips, see **Check-in** from Session 2. Help clients see patterns in their use or change strategies: "What strategies from last week's **Triggers, Consequences and Alternatives** exercise did you try?" "How have these last few weeks gone for you — better, worse or about the same?" Help clients to use strategies other than avoidance: "Avoiding triggers is the first step for a lot of people. What are the good things and not-so-good things about doing that?" "What is the next step?"
☐ 2. Introduce the **Things That Are Important to Me** exercise.	"This exercise is about finding out what you want out of your life. Read through the whole list and choose the top ten things that are important to you or that you want to work towards." (For larger groups, have them pick out ten, but discuss only the top two or three items.) Affirmation: "Looks like you want to make some changes in your life and that you know what you want." Make steps towards goals more concrete: "When you picture yourself doing that, what are you doing? What are the steps to get there?" Look at the impact of drug use on achievement of goals: "Where do drugs fit into your goals?" "Where were you six months ago in relation to your goals? "Where do you see yourself six months from now?" "What about your use?"

Guidelines for the counsellor	Tips on what to do with or say to the client
❑ 3. Wrap up.	Integrating life goals. "What is one thing you can do this week that would help you move a step closer to one of your life goals?"

Progress Note
for Session 3:
Things that are important to me

• • • • • •

NAME: _____   FILE#: _____   SESSION DATE: _____

❏ Client Cancelled (specify action plan)   Action Plan: _____
❏ No Show (specify action plan)   _____
❏ Clinician Cancelled (specify action plan) _____

❏ Attended Session 3 of the *First Contact* program.

This session was conducted in the following format: ❏ Individual   ❏ Group

This session covered the following (check one box):

Covered	Not Covered	
❏	❏	Client completed **Check-in** and discussed progress over the last week.
❏	❏	Client was helped by counsellor(s) and group to explore strategies to deal with high-risk situations.
❏	❏	Counsellor(s) introduced **Things That Are Important to Me** exercise.
❏	❏	Client completed and discussed the **Things That Are Important to Me** exercise.
❏	❏	Explored impact of drug use on life goals.
❏	❏	Asked client to identify one step towards life goal over the next week(s).
❏	❏	Asked client(s) to try one alternative to drug use strategy over the next week.
❏	❏	Reviewed today's group experience.

Substance Use Since Last Session: ❏ Abstinent   ❏ Non-Abstinent
Substances/Frequency/Quantity:_____
Drug Use Goal(s):
Participation in Group: ❏ Low   ❏ Moderate   ❏ High
Therapists at this session were (for group only):
Outcome of Session:
❏ Next Session Scheduled for: _____
❏ Treatment Terminated (client initiated)*
❏ Treatment Terminated (clinician initiated)*   * discharge summary req'd
Additional Notes:

_____   _____
Signature/Credentials   Date

Check-in

I USED OR THOUGHT ABOUT USING ON...

I WANTED TO USE...

MY GOALS

WHEN I THOUGHT ABOUT USING, I...

Monday

Tuesday

Wednesday

Thursday

Friday

Saturday

Sunday

- ☐ When I felt the need to cope
- ☐ When I just wanted to have fun
- ☐ Out of habit
- ☐ Other

My goals for the next week are:

- ☐ Not to use
- ☐ Reduced use
- ☐ Work on one of my life goals
- ☐ Other

- ☐ Used
- ☐ Did something else
- ☐ Thought about consequences
- ☐ Avoided using
- ☐ Other

My week was

0	5	10
lousy	OK	fantastic

Things that are important to me

- - - - -

Please read through the whole list and choose the top 10 things that are important to you.

❑ **Friends**
to have close, supportive friends

❑ **Hope**
to maintain a positive and optimistic outlook

❑ **Self-esteem**
to like myself just as I am

❑ **Achievement**
to accomplish and achieve

❑ **Comfort**
to have a pleasant, enjoyable life

❑ **Fame**
to be known and recognized

❑ **Humour**
to see the humorous side of myself and the world

❑ **Loved**
to be loved by those close to me

❑ **Romance**
to have an intense, exciting love relationship

❑ **Self-knowledge**
to have a deep, honest understanding of myself

❑ **Acceptance**
to fit in with others

❑ **Attractiveness**
to be physically attractive

❑ **Dependability**
to be reliable and trustworthy

❑ **Flexibility**
to adjust to new or unusual situations easily

❑ **Fun**
to play and have fun

❑ **Health**
to be physically well and healthy

❑ **Independence**
to be free from dependence on others

❑ **Leisure**
to take time to relax and enjoy

❑ **Loving**
to give love to others

❑ **Moderation**
to avoid excesses and find a middle ground

❑ **Monogamy**
to have one close, loving relationship

❑ **Pleasure**
to feel good

❑ **Popularity**
to be well liked by many people

❑ **Self-control**
to be disciplined and govern my own actions

❑ **Sexuality**
to have an active and satisfying sex life

❑ **Wealth**
to have plenty of money

❑ **Contribution**
to make a contribution that will endure

❑ **Creativity**
to have new and original ideas

- **Faithfulness**
  to be loyal and reliable in relationships

- **Family**
  to have a happy, loving family

- **God's will**
  to seek and obey the will of God

- **Inner peace**
  to experience personal peace

- **Knowledge**
  to learn and possess valuable knowledge

- **Orderliness**
  to have a life that is well ordered and organized

- **Realism**
  to see and act realistically and practically

- **Safety**
  to be safe and secure

- **Simplicity**
  to live life simply, with minimal needs

- **Spirituality**
  to grow spiritually

- **Tolerance**
  to accept and respect those different from me

- **Accuracy**
  to be correct in my opinions and actions

- **Adventure**
  to have new and exciting experiences

- **Courtesy**
  to be polite and considerate to others

- **Forgiveness**
  to be forgiving of others

- **Industry**
  to work hard and well at my life tasks

- **Logic**
  to live rationally and sensibly

- **Stability**
  to have a life that stays fairly consistent

Top 10 Ways of Achieving Your Goals

1. Desire: choose a goal that you really want to achieve.

2. Belief: choose a goal that is challenging but realistic, and one that you believe you can achieve.

3. Benefits: list the benefits that will come from achieving your goal — the more benefits, the more motivated and persistent you will be.

4. Obstacles: identify some of the obstacles and think about how you will deal with them — there are always obstacles to achieving a worthwhile goal.

5. Knowledge: find out what you need to know to achieve your goal.

6. People: identify the people who can help you achieve your goal.

7. Current Status: figure out where you are now on your way to achieving your goal — for example, if you want to improve your self-esteem, ask yourself, on a scale of 1 to 10, "where am I now? — what one small step can I take to move a little closer to my goal?"

8. Plan: make a plan, break things down into small manageable steps, make the steps concrete and be willing to revise your plan. Remember, no first plan is perfect.

9. Timeline: set an overall timeline for when you want to achieve your goal. Then think about how much time it will take to complete the first step.

10. Persistence: keep in mind that mistakes and disappointments can occur, but that you can make it. It's not always smooth sailing to your goals.

Adapted from Miller, W. R., & C'deBaca, J. (1994).

Session

4 Stages of change

Session 4
Stages of change

<table>
<tr><td>

Materials needed

Counsellor's materials
1. Goals for Session 4: Stages of Change
2. Checklist for Session 4: Stages of Change
3. Progress Note for Session 4: Stages of Change

Client handouts
1. Check-in
2. Stages of Change

</td></tr>
</table>

Stages of Change (Prochaska et. al., 1992)	Phrases used in *First Contact's* Stages of Change exercise
Precontemplation	I'm not interested in changing
Contemplation	Should I stay or should I go?
Preparation	Getting ready
Action	I'm breaking away
Maintenance	I'm staying the course
Relapse	I've slipped off course
Permanent change	I've discovered a whole new world

REVIEW OF CHANGE PROCESS

Session 4 is the last session in the *First Contact* program. Consequently, the primary goals for clients in this session are to review progress and affirm whatever positive changes have taken place in their lives (even if it were only increased awareness) and, if the counsellor is leading a *First Contact* group, to review the group process and emphasize the sharing and support that have occurred. Because many of these young clients have difficulty completing things, it is also worthwhile to acknowledge their success in completing the *First Contact* program. Show that you recognize the motivation and courage that it takes for them to examine the impact of use on their lives.

The **Stages of Change** exercise is included to increase clients' understanding of change as a process and to take a long-term perspective on change. The **Stages of Change** exercise does not include the original terms used by Prochaska et al. (1992). Instead, the terms for the stages have been modified to reflect the space journey theme depicted in the illustrations, using everyday language that is more appealing to young clients.

Clients are asked to identify what stage they were in when they started *First Contact* and where they are now. This exercise highlights the changes that have occurred and what clients did to make those changes. It is also helpful to talk about concrete ways to maintain gains and to get to the next stage, if clients are not in the maintenance stage already.

TREATMENT NEEDS AND OPTIONS FOR THE FUTURE

This session is also the time to talk with the client about treatment needs after *First Contact*. The recommended treatment plan will depend on the characteristics of the client, the response to treatment, and the options available. For those who have responded well and have no other urgent treatment needs, continuing care is a common suggestion. For those with additional needs, individual, family or specific skills (e.g., anger management) treatment should also be considered. For those who have not responded to treatment, case management and referral to a more intensive intervention (e.g., community day program) may be suggested.

Goals
for Session 4: Stages of change

➊ Review progress, emphasize success, especially barriers to change.

➋ Continue to discuss use goals in the context of "life goals."

➌ Discuss future treatment planning.

➍ Review *First Contact* treatment and changes made in all life areas.

➎ For groups, review group process — emphasize sharing in group as positive risk-taking.

➏ Acknowledge completion of *First Contact* cycle (i.e., success and achievement).

➐ Complete the **Stages of Change** exercise.
Goals:
   a. Increase awareness of change as a process.
   b. Identify clients' stage of change.
   c. Increase concrete changes made during *First Contact* treatment.
   d. Explore more concrete ways of getting to the next stage of change.

Checklist
for Session 4: Stages of change

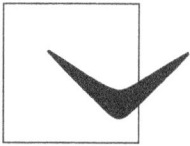

Guidelines for the counsellor	Tips on what to do with or say to the client
❑ 1. **Check-in.**	Discuss progress over the past week: For tips, see **Check-in** from Session 2. Help clients to consolidate change: "Over the course of the last four weeks, what strategies have been the most helpful?" "Is this pattern of use (or abstinence) something you can keep up?"
❑ 2. Introduce **Stages of Change** exercise.	Review and consolidate progress: "This exercise is a way of figuring out where you are. Change is like taking a journey. Some people aren't interested in making the journey at all. Others are uncertain and ask themselves, 'should I stay or should I go?' Others are already prepared to take off... etc. Look over these statements and tell us: Where were you when you came in? Where are you now? What led to the change (if any)? What are the next steps (i.e. coping strategies, treatment referrals)?"
❑ 3. Discuss additional treatment options.	Look at future treatment planning: "What kind of additional help might be useful at this point? What would you like to work on in the next month or two?"
❑ 4. Wrap up.	Highlight changes and progress, review treatment process, and obtain feedback: "What did you think about being here for the past four weeks?" "What was the first group session like for you?" "How did things change for you in the group over the four weeks?" (Emphasize ability to stick with it despite initial discomfort.) "What was most helpful about the treatment?" "Do you have any suggestions on how to improve these groups?"

Progress Note
for Session 4:
Stages of change

● ● ● ● ● ●

NAME: _____   FILE#: _____   SESSION DATE: _____

❑ Client Cancelled (specify action plan)   Action Plan: _____
❑ No Show (specify action plan)   _____
❑ Clinician Cancelled (specify action plan) _____

❑ Attended Session 4 of the *First Contact* program.

This session was conducted in the following format: ❑ Individual   ❑ Group

This session covered the following (check one box):

Covered	Not Covered	
❑	❑	Client completed **Check-in** and discussed progress over the last week.
❑	❑	Client was helped by counsellor(s) and group to review strategies to deal with high-risk situations.
❑	❑	Counsellor(s) introduced **Stages of Change** exercise.
❑	❑	Client completed and discussed the **Stages of Change** exercise.
❑	❑	Explored readiness, motivation and commitment toward changing drug use.
❑	❑	Discussed what is needed to maintain change or reach current goals (i.e., "next steps").
❑	❑	Asked client(s) about their group experience over the past four weeks. Elicited suggestions for improving group experience.

Substance Use Since Last Session: ❑ Abstinent   ❑ Non-Abstinent

Substances/Frequency/Quantity: _____

Drug Use Goal(s):

Participation in Group: ❑ Low   ❑ Moderate   ❑ High

Therapists at this session were (for group only):

Outcome of Session:

❑ Next Session Scheduled for: _____

❑ Treatment Completed*

❑ Treatment Terminated (client initiated)*

❑ Treatment Terminated (clinician initiated)*   *discharge summary req'd

Additional Notes:

_____   _____
Signature/Credentials   Date

Check-in

I USED OR THOUGHT ABOUT USING ON…

Monday

Tuesday

Wednesday

Thursday

Friday

Saturday

Sunday

I WANTED TO USE…

☐ When I felt the need to cope

☐ When I just wanted to have fun

☐ Out of habit

☐ Other

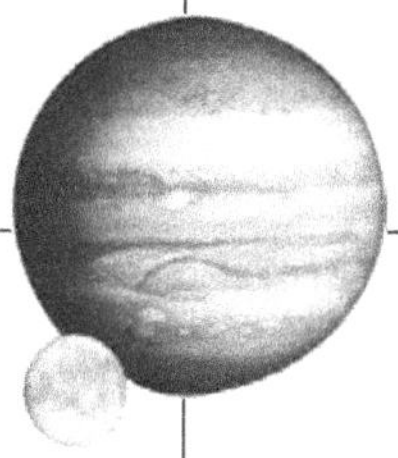

My goals for the next week are:

☐ Not to use

☐ Reduced use

☐ Work on one of my life goals

☐ Other

MY GOALS

☐ Used

☐ Did something else

☐ Thought about consequences

☐ Avoided using

☐ Other

WHEN I THOUGHT ABOUT USING, I…

0	5	10

My week was

lousy   OK   fantastic

Stages of Change

1 I'm not interested in changing

2 Should I stay or should I go?
(thinking about change)

3 Getting ready

4 I'm breaking away
(making a change)

5 I'm staying the course

I've slipped off course

6 I've discovered a whole new world

Adapted from Prochaska, DiClemente & Rychtarik (1992).

References

Addiction Research Foundation * (1991). *Youth and Drugs: An Education Package for Professionals.* Toronto, Ontario: Addiction Research Foundation.

Berg, I. K. (1995). Solution-focused brief therapy with substance abusers. In A. M. Washton (Ed.) *Psychotherapy and Substance Abuse.* New York: Guilford Press.

Bien, T. H., Miller, W. R., & Tonigan, J. S. (1993). Brief interventions for alcohol problems: a review. *Addiction*, 88:3, 15-36.

DiClemente, C. C., & Hughes, S. O. (1990). Stages of change profiles in outpatient alcoholism treatment. *Journal of Substance Abuse*, 2, 217-235.

Janis, I. L., & Mann, L. (1977). Decision-making: A psychological analysis of conflict, choice, and commitment. New York: Free Press.

Lawendowski, L. A. (1998). A motivational intervention for adolescent smokers. *Preventive Medicine*, 27, A39-A46.

Marlatt, G. A., & Gordon, J. R. (1985). *Relapse Prevention.* New York: Guilford Press.

Miller, W. R. (1999). *Personal Communication at the Motivational Interviewing and Brief Negotiation Workshop.* Albuquerque, New Mexico, January 8-11, 1999.

Miller, W. R., & C'deBaca, J. (1994). Quantum change: Toward a psychology of transformation. In T. Heatherton & J. Weinberger (Eds.), *Can personality change?* (pp. 253-280). Washington, DC: American Psychological Association.

Miller, W. R., & Rollnick, S. (1991). *Motivational Interviewing: Preparing People to Change Addictive Behaviour.* New York: Guilford.

Miller, W. R., & Rollnick, S. (1998). *Motivational Interviewing video series.* Albuquerque, NM: Horizon West Productions.

Miller, W. R., Zweben, A., DiClemente, C. C., & Rychtarik, R. G. (1995). *Motivational Enhancement Therapy.* Washington, D.C.: National Institute of Health.

Ontario Ministry of Health. (1995). *Ontario Health Survey 1990: Mental Health Supplement: User's Guide Vol. 1 Documentation.* Toronto: Ontario Ministry of Health.

Prochaska, J. O., DiClemente, C. C., & Norcross, J. C. (1992). In search of how people change. *American Psychologist*, 47, 1102-1114.

Sanchez-Craig, M, Annis, H. M., Bornet, A. R., & MacDonald, K. R. (1984). Random assignment to abstinence and controlled drinking: Evaluation of a cognitive-behavioural program for problem drinkers. *Journal of Consulting and Clinical Psychology*, 52, 390-403

Schulman, L. (1999) *The Skills of Helping Individuals, Families, Groups and Communities,* 4th edition. Itasca, Ill: F.E. Peacock Publications.

Sobell, M. B., & Sobell, L. C. (1993). *Problem Drinkers: Guided Self-change Treatment.* New York: Guilford Press.

Stark, M. J. (1992). Dropping out of substance abuse treatment: A clinically oriented review. *Clinical Psychology Review*, 12, 93-116.

Statistics Canada. (1994). *Microdata User's Guide: Canada's Alcohol and Other Drugs Survey.* Ottawa, Canada: Statistics Canada, Special Surveys Division.

Wilkinson, D. A., & Martin, G. A. (1983). Experimental comparison of behavioural treatments of multiple drug abuse: Brief outpatient self-control training and two broad spectrum residential treatments. Paper presented at the 17th Annual Convention of the Association for the Advancement of Behavior Therapy, Washington, D.C.

* The Addiction Research Foundation is now a division of the Centre for Addiction and Mental Health.

www.ingramcontent.com/pod-product-compliance
Lightning Source LLC
Chambersburg PA
CBHW080937040426
42443CB00015B/3447

9 780888 683557